GREAT BRIXTON.

51.4630° N
00.1060° W

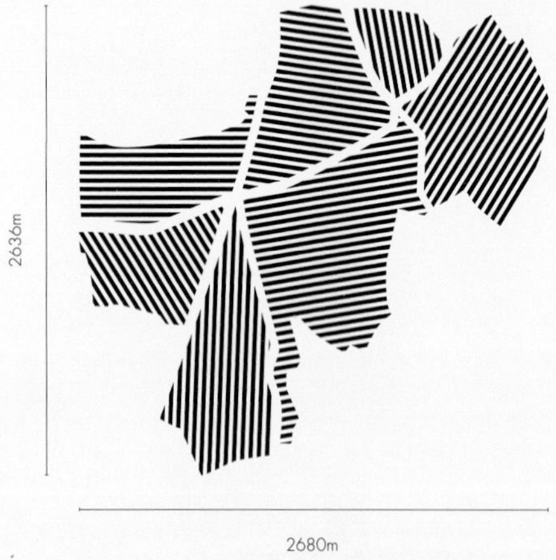

2636m

2680m

Approximate scale of the capital of South London in metres.

GREAT BRIXTON.

World famous, sometimes infamous.

This book is the collective story of one of the most vibrant communities in the UK. We invited everyone who knows and loves Brixton to share images of what makes it great, with the simple aim of preserving its unique diversity in print.

Over the year we received thousands of pictures. We thank everyone for their generous contributions. The final 273 images form their own community: they start conversations, telling overlapping, hilarious and heartfelt stories. From headline events to the rituals of daily life, these are images captured by the people who lived these moments.

This book is dedicated not only to the image-makers, but to all the people of Brixton past and present who fill these photographs with life.

Welcome to Great Brixton.

Iceland's staff staircase. 1993. ▸

THE FUTURE BEGINS
'HERE' WITH US
WELCOME TO
BRIXTON

Bob Marley Way, off Mayall Road.

Foot Locker post-riots. 2011.

Two amazing ladies: my grandma and godmother. Taken by my dad in the early 90s before I was born.

This Brixtonite shows that the many are more powerful than the few. This isn't an act of defiance, but a gesture of power to the people.

RIP Madiba wall. Artwork by Jon Daniels. Windrush Square. 2013.

Nelson Mandela at Brixton Recreation Centre. 1996. ▸

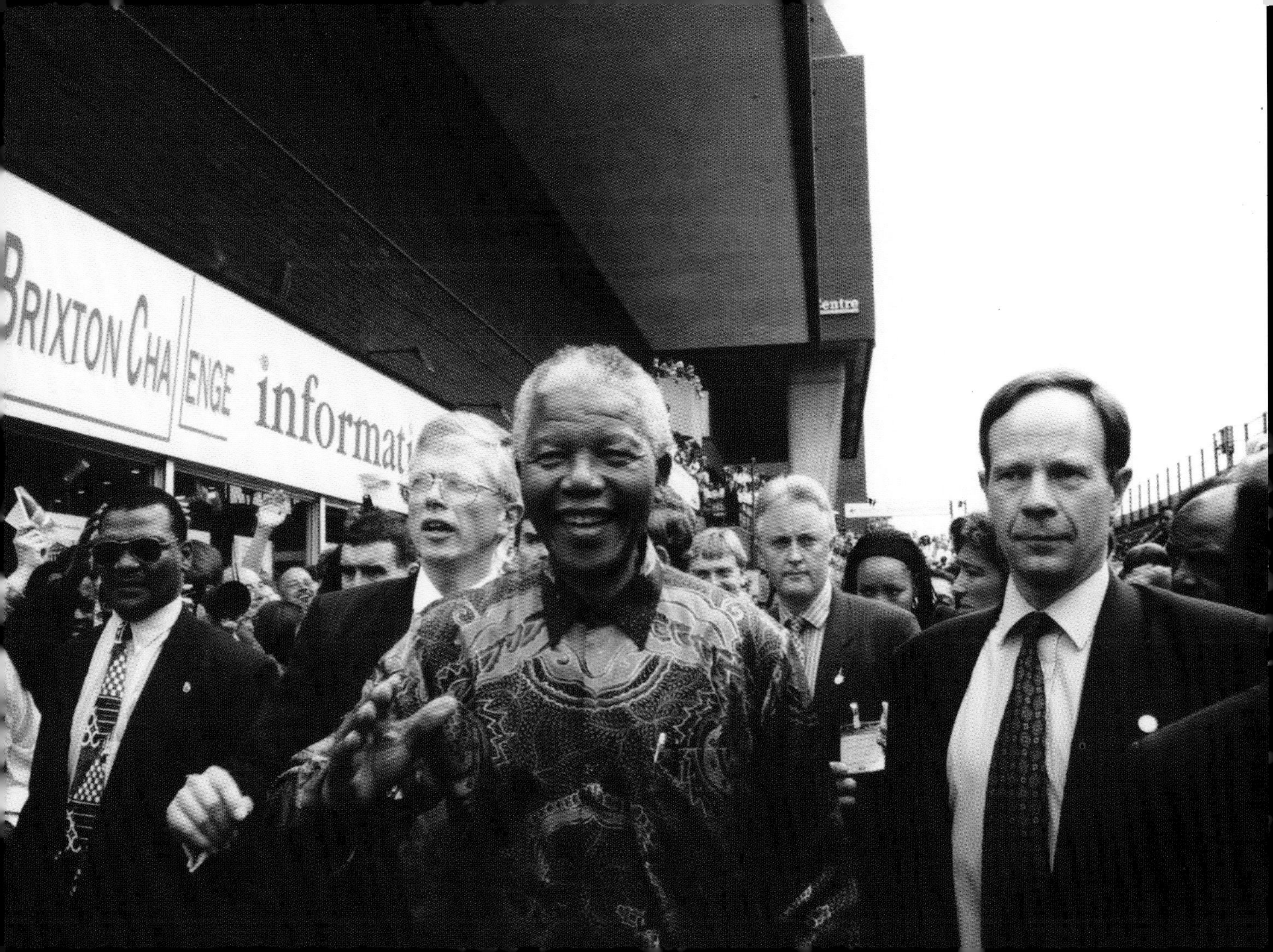

BRIXTON CHA
LENGE
informati
Centre

I ♥ DIVERSITY
I ♥ CREATIVITY
I ♥ BRIXTON
BIG HUGS
AM XXX
LAURA SAYS
"IT'S ALL ABOUT BRIKKY"
I ♥ BRIXTON

We Love Brixton was formed by local residents and business owners as a direct response to the 2011 riots.

Coming here as a child was like a trip to a theme park. The face of Brixton may change, but not the heart.

◀ 'We love Brixton', inspired notes of love.

The only road in the UK named after the Pan-African leader.

Homage to history and music. Market Row. 2001. ▸

Confessions of a Black Woman
PRINCE JAZZ
IN THE 70s
BIRMINGHAM
SAT. 7TH APRIL 2001
UNIVERSITY OF DUB
A ROOTS AND DUBZ DANCE
ABA-SHANTI-I
JAH-TUBBY'S
IRATION STEPPA'S
ON FRIDAY 4th MAY 2001
Tuesdays
BIG BAMKOO
HON. MARCUS "MESSIAH" GARVEY

The Family Car. Effra Parade.

Lady in the entrance to Brixton Village from Atlantic Road. ▶

We Do Watch
Batteries &
Straps
Digice
top u
Lebara

Long may the larger-than-life characters of the neighbourhood continue to make it a great place to live.

Bringing home the shopping behind Woolworths. Electric Lane.

Panoramic view from Lambeth Town Hall looking southeast. 1936. ▶

TATE
LIBRARY
FREE
PRESS
BOVRIL
IS THE POWER OF BEEF
CAPSTAN
ALE
CYCLE
RACING
BOOK HERE
FOR
SOUTHDOWN
LONDON
COASTAL
Esso
NO
PRIVATE
CARS
SUPPLIED
Esso

DAILY TO ALL SEASIDE RESORTS
and Saturday Afternoon Services
BOOKING OFFICE FOR
ORANGE LUXURY COACHES
LONDON COASTAL COACHES
SOUTH DOWN EAST KENT
RAVEL BY COACH
S CHEAPER!
NO
RIVATE
CARS
PPLIED
ESSO
33

View of Brixton Road, taken from a location that today would be above Brixton Tube Station. ▶

BON MARCHE
BONMARCHE
TAILORING & OUTFITTING
WALLACE HUGHES
THE BRIXTON DRAPER
ORROMS BOOTS
CLARK & SON
S.A.NEWMAN
THE BRIXTON TAILOR
H.FORD & Co Ld
452 BRIXTON Rd
The Old Established High-Class Butchers
WINES & ALES
RESTAURANT
SANDERS & COMPANY
PINK'S MARMALADE
TEAS
The U.S.A. Studios Branches
KENNINGTON THEATRE
PEARS
Vi-Cocoa
NEIGHBOUR'S
WESTON & SONS
BOUQUETS

Brixton Road, down past the railway bridge, Rush Common tapers to a point at what is now The Beehive.

View of the corner of Brixton Road and Acre Lane. ▶

ISAAC WALTON & CO LTD
INDIAN OUTFITS
MOTOR OUTFITS
ATHLETIC OUTFITS
520 ISAAC WALTON & Co Ltd 518
BESPOKE TAILORING
BOYS' SCHOOL OUTFITS
BESPOKE TAILORING
BOYS' SCHOOL OUTFITS
SCHWEPPES
BRITISH
Pears
GENERAL
BRIXTON & CAMDEN TOWN
HAMPTONS Carpets Curtains
GENERAL
SINGER
SEWING MACHINES
Brixton Road, S.W.
2437

Reflections. From the butchers, Atlantic Road. 2007.

The king of Brixton.

The vibrancy of Brixton.

I'd like to think that the two men were long lost friends, and they had reunited that day on Brixton Road road as the world walked by.

Atlantic Road.

This photo is somewhat elegant. The otherwise so busy arches appear peaceful.

Brixton Road.

Foot Locker post-riots. 2011.

Street art meets street life on Atlantic Road at Brixton Splash 2015. A real community event.

◀ Gospel singers on Brixton Road.

Taken at Reclaim Brixton, this image captures a joyful moment of pride and celebration of a local resident.

Style and diversity at every turn on Brixton Station Road. A source of sartorial inspiration.

Saturday Night Car. Atlantic Road.

Enjoying Brixton Splash. An annual all-singing, all-dancing celebration of culture and community. ▶

Michael Jordan with the Brixton Topcats. Brixton Recreation Centre. 1985. ▶

BRIXTON
BASKETBALL
CLUB

BODYBRITE
Jamaica
2163
M&S

Paul Marriott is Mr Brixton Bolt, the only person to win three consecutive years.

And the award for best costume goes to… Josh Lindo.

Kids' categories from under-3s upwards always receive the biggest cheers from spectators.

The T-shirt says it all!

◀ Enjoying Brixton Splash. While an independent Jamaica turns 50 and Usain Bolt wins 100m & 200m Gold at the London Olympics.

'SW2 World Cup' in Brockwell Park. We pick children to represent their parents' country of origin.

Local under-10s derby against Stockwell Community FC in Slade Gardens. 2013-2014 season.

Brockwell Lido. 2013.

Brockwell Lido. 2014.

Brockwell Park BMX track. 2013.

Children enjoying themselves in Brixton Skatepark.

GRAND BILLIARD
HORSE
SALOON

The second hand market. Brixton Station Road. 1992.

Between customers.

Dominoes in Brockwell Park.

Draughts in Negusa Negast, the Rastafarian Community Centre in St Agnes Place Squat. 2006.

◂ The White Horse on the corner of Loughborough Road and Brixton Road. Now Brixton Jamm.

Grantham Road Estate in the 1980s.

Winners, 'Car Free Day', Coldharbour Lane, organised by Brixton Cycles. 2000. ▸

SPECIALIZED
LARRY
HOLMIE AGENCY
TEL 071-737 6401
FAX 071-733 6591
BRIXTON
071 733 6055
1

Lambeth Country Show. Brockwell Park. 1998.

A Saturday in Brixton Market. 1996.

Brockwell Park. 2015.

Time out on the wall. 1980s. ▸

Brockwell Park. 2013.

Jumping fences. 1990. ▸

Enjoying the summer sun in the fountain. Windrush Square.

Winds That Rush On.

From Manisa's window. Crownstone Court. 1993.

007 Boy. Brockwell Park.

◀ After school. Brixton Road. 2005.

Atlantic Road. 2013.

Brixton Market has always been great value compared to the high street. The designs are often unique.

◀ Lambeth Country Show. 2014.

CEASEFIRE

No Frills
APRIL FOOLS
at the
LOBSTER CLUB
the

Seen from my window: a response to another knife crime attack. Vining Street. 2009.

◂ Art is political and social. Brixton Station Road. 1996.

Peace
Reign
the
World
POLICE
AMC
POLICE POLICE
GUINNESS STOP
EVICTION

Ricky Bishop, died 2001 in custody at Brixton police station. His family is still fighting for justice.

St Agnes Place squat evictions left 150 people homeless and 21 houses demolished. 2005.

◂ An expression of peace at the Reclaim Brixton event. 2015.

We Love Brixton. Artwork by Gnasher. Windrush Square.

We Love Brixton. Artwork by Benjamin Wachenje. Windrush Square.

A defiant youth steadfastly faces police lines during Brixton riots following the Swamp 81 operation. 1981. ▶

A local resident looks on as riot police sweep through the streets of Brixton during rioting. 1981.

◀ The front line. Railton Road. Rioting overwhelmed police after a stabbing during the Swamp 81 operation targeting black youth

Flying bomb strikes Acre Lane, killing 72 people. 1944.

Brixton street awaiting demolition.

Aftermath of the1981 uprising on the corner of Railton Road.

Foxtons: a regular outlet for anti-gentrification anger. Reclaim Brixton event.

Off Effra Parade, a shop burned out during the 1981 uprising.

Another casualty of the 1981 uprising.

Gresham Road. Reclaim Brixton. April 2015.

An anti-gentrification protest with marchers and police in attendance - both of whom are likely affected by very high house prices in Brixton. ▸

MP
MP
F H
EG

Budget Carpets grass. Atlantic Road.

◀ Patrolling the hillside in Brockwell Park.

Brixton stand with GAZA

Young Barack and Michelle on vinyl. Windrush Square.

◀ Brixton foreign policy. Brixton Water Lane.

82-84 Atlantic Road. c.1902. ▶

RNISHER
ON
EASY
TERMS
ANKERSON BROS.

THE BRIXTON FRUIT MARKET

Early morning, the stallholders are busy setting up. Spot the hats - a very stylish father and son.

Milk delivery cart in Electric Avenue.

ONE

THE WIG BAZAAR
SPECIALISTS
IN WIGS &
HAIR EXTENSIONS
THE WIG BAZAAR
57
KUMASI MARKET
DAGONS
DAGONS
Est. 1953

Atlantic Road has long been famed for its butchers, fishmongers and grocers.

A Saturday in Brixton Market. Electric Avenue. 1996.

Brixton Cycles 'thought for the day'. Stockwell Road.

Brixton Cycles: keeping wheels turning since 1983. Stockwell Road.

◀ 'Granville Arcade' shortly before it began to be revitalised.

The Grosvenor, one of many local pubs and music venues lost by gentrification and developers.

The last folk night at the Grosvenor.

Woolworths' first London store opened in Brixton in 1910, closing in 2009 after the company's collapse.

We hoped to bring as much life and colour to the people of Brixton with our Christmas advent calendar.

A Sunday morning with meaning. Electric Avenue. 1993.

Strolling.

Walking towards Stockwell.

A man pauses in front of the derelict Brady's Pub (now Wahaca). Atlantic Road. 2009.

'Costos', unique raconteur of the Phoenix Café. Coldharbour Lane. 1992.

The Granville Arcade Market.

Still smiling at the Pie and Mash Shop.

Cows' feet only 43p.

Electric Avenue from Brixton Road. Christmas. 1908.

The secret tunnel of small local shops that connects Brixton high street to the market. Reliance Arcade.

Electric Avenue from Brixton Road. Christmas. 1909. ▶

Colourful traders and their colourful produce make Brixton Market a vibrant centre of the community.

Brixton Village: a vibrant and unique space enriched by a strong sense of community and belonging.

George James (Raz Napthalie), leader and founder of the Food Growing & Food Awareness program.

This environmental project was awarded 'The Community Group BTCV Green Heroes Award'. 2007.

Electric Avenue butcher.

Portuguese Deli in festive spirit. Atlantic Road.

Taken by my mum, I hope we'll look back in several years and see the same kind of shops we do today.

Well-established trades and niche goods find a home in the dusky and atmospheric Reliance Acrade.

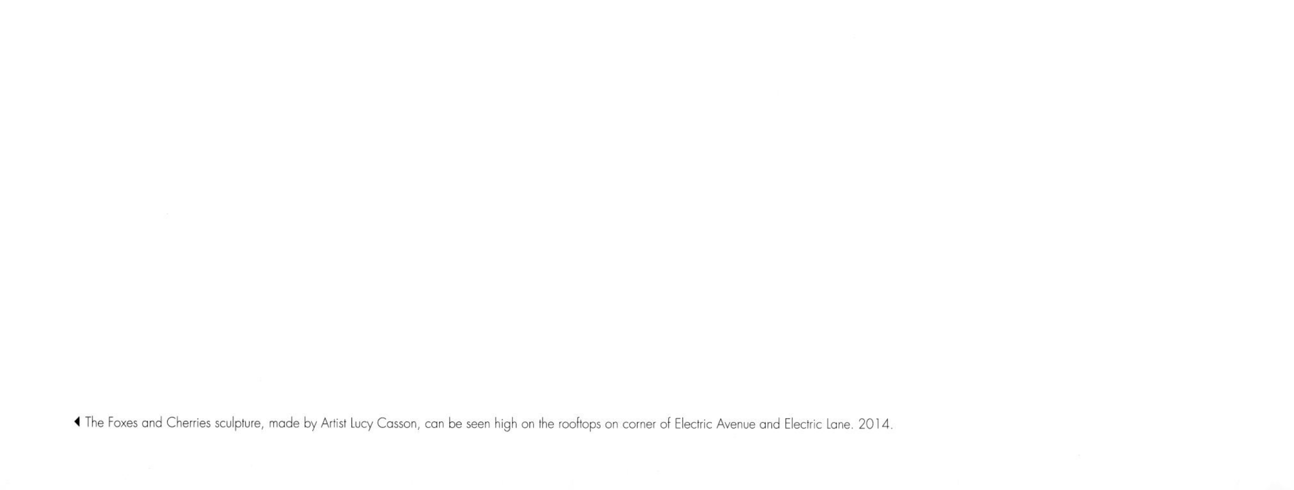

◀ The Foxes and Cherries sculpture, made by Artist Lucy Casson, can be seen high on the rooftops on corner of Electric Avenue and Electric Lane. 2014.

Brixton Station. Facing Pope's Road. The houses to the left are now the site of Pop Brixton.

The Carlton Club. Granville Arcade/ Brixton Village was to be built here. To the right, Walton Lodge Laundry. ▶

WALTON
LODGE
CARLTON CLUB
WALTON LODGE
SANITARY STEAM LAUNDRY
SANITARY
TEAM LAUNDRY.
SANITARY
LAUNDRY.

A view of Electric Avenue from Brixton Road. Notice the pharmacy on the corner.

Atlantic Road from its junction with Pope's Road. The white building in the background is now The Dogstar.

#SaveBrixtonArches activist DJ BlondeZilla wearing an apt top with message a for those behind the evictions.

Brixton is a laid-back place. It's not just hipsters who are the cool cats in Brixton Village.

Shutter painted by PINS Artist, kicking off #SaveBrixtonArches, supporting deli owner Jo Cardoso and family. ▶

A.&C. CO. CONTINENTAL GROCERS.
OUR HEART IS HERE!
#PINSARTIST

Another shop closes down. Market Row. 2005.

The market is never boring. There is always something interesting to see and discover. In this case, wigs.

Wearing (we are in) Jamaica.

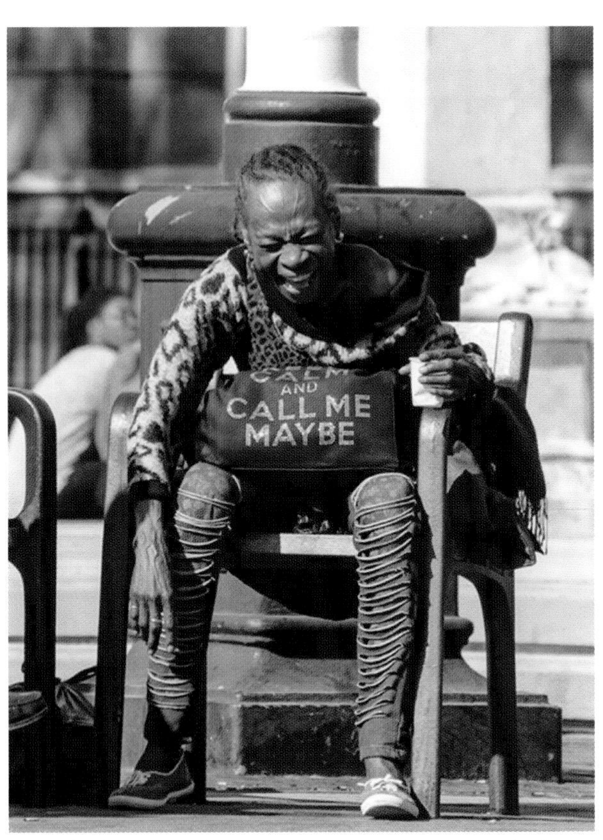

A moment of laughter brought on by the third or fourth Red Stripe… Well it was a warm day after all!

opean Hair Styles
3 4173
BAN

◀ A portrait of portraits. Harry Jacob's portrait studio. Landor Road. 1994.

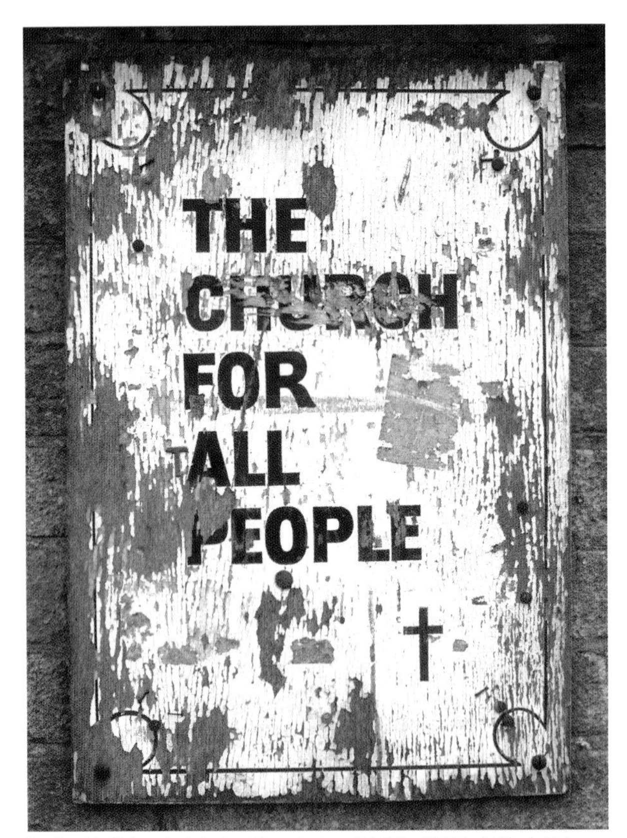

The Church for (T)all people. A cheeky addition to the sign outside Brixton Hill Methodist Church. Brixton.

Simple and surreal. A symbolic defence of Brixton.

Slade Gardens. Part of Brixton's beautiful collection of murals.

Brixton Windmill Mural fully restored. Blenheim Gardens Estate. 2015.

The Brixton Pound reconnects us with our local community and gives us the courage and ability to use our money positively. Oh, and David Bowie, obvs.

Artist paints a mural dedicated to the former Brixton resident himself. ▸

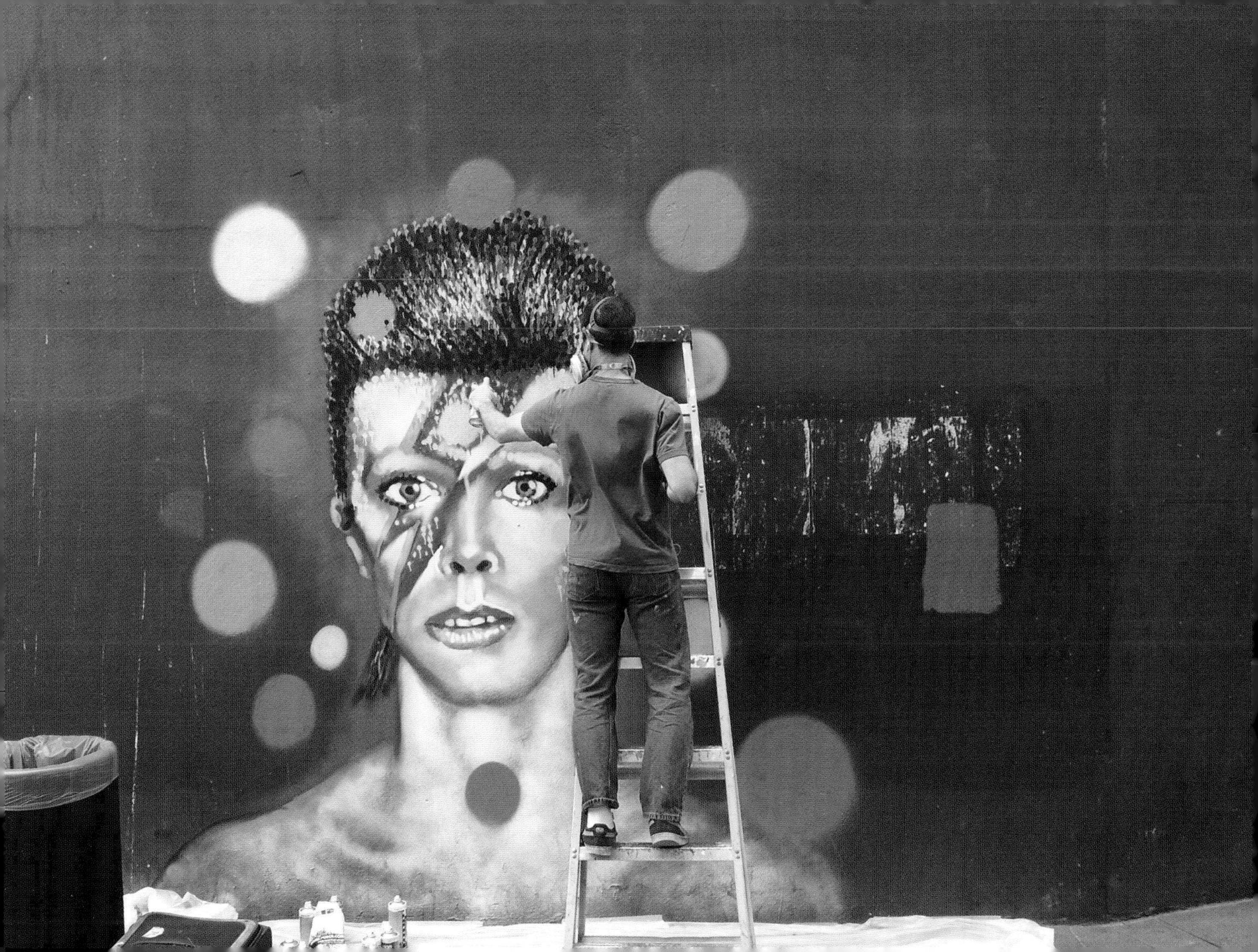

Anonymous art: A portrait in honour of Michael Jackson? Atlantic Road. 2009.

A tribute to Jam Master Jay. Granville Arcade. 2006. ▶

R.I.P JAM MASTER JAY 1965 -2002
"the turntables might wobble but they dont fall down'
RUN DMC

Big Splash Street Mural in Glenelg Road. Created by Christine Thomas. 1985.

Mauleverer Road Mural. Created by Jane Gifford and Ruth Bench. 1983.

When I see this painting in Brixton I feel like I'm home. It's been a part of Brixton for so many years. It is singularly Brixton.

Gypsy Bird. Railton Road.

Boxing Day. Somerleyton Passage. 2014.

This is that piece my friends did in Brixton in about 1986-ish. Freshly sprayed - the cans used are on the floor. It was on St Saviour's Road.

A chalked message. The back wall of the Dog Star. Vining Street. 2008.

ZACCAI 1ST B'DAY
ZACCAI MEANS PURE & JUST
LOVE THE LIFE YOU LIVE
LIVE THE LIFE YOU LOVE
ONE HEART ONE LOVE ONE LIFE
OUT OF MANY WE

JAMAICA AVENUE LTD
CLOSING
DOWN-SALE
FOR
REALOCATION
CLOSINGDOWN
SALE SALE
FOR
REALOCATION

Mr Biggs on Atlantic Road was the definition of bits and bobs. With patience, you could find anything here.

Very direct marketing. Railton Road.

◂ 'Sale Sale' at men's clothing outlet. Atlantic Road. 2006.

Rubbish philosophy. Windrush Square.

Taken when I was in between jobs. Work did indeed start soon for me!

Only Bargains. Atlantic Road. 2006

Untitled. Barrington Road.

Fortified front door at St Agnes Place squat, showing the constant fear of eviction.

Down but not out.

One of the many shop frontages vandalised in the 2011 riots.

Business As Usual (we're not closed).

On the way home.

I'm no fan of Big Box Retail, so I must admit to a certain degree of schadenfreude when I took this picture. Still, I did buy my kettle there. ▶

currys

Coldharbour Lane. Leather goods.

The former Howes Cash & Carry. Atlantic Road. 2001.

MARKS & SPENCER LTD
ORIGINAL PENNY BAZAAR.
ADMISSION FREE
MARKS
AND
SPENCER
MARKS
AND
SPENCER
LIMITED

Workers Newspaper. Read all about it.

◀ M&S have now operated in Brixton for over 100 years. Here, the original Marks and Spencers site. Atlantic Road. 1920s.

My family, godmother and grandma visiting from Greenock, Scotland. Outside Brixton Wholefoods, where my dad worked before I was born.

Serving the community since 1982. Atlantic Road. ▶

Brixton Wholefoods
59
(transatlantic)
0207·737·2210

blitz
Vaico
GENTRIFICATION ART
NO THANKS!

Home
CARLTON

Brixton Buzz's April Fools renaming Brixton as Clapham East, a response to gentrification. Many were fooled.

Echoes of the 1980s riots.

Reclaim Brixton. Windrush Square. 2015.

Sorry Tarquin. Saltoun Road.

◂ Carlton Mansions was one of Brixton's longest-running housing co-ops before eviction by Lambeth Council. 2014.

Atlantic Road. Brixton. May 2015.

Atlantic Road. Brixton. March 2015.

Waiting for Mum. ▶

LAMBETH
Construction
Services
Telephone 274 7722
SMASH H BLOCK

RITZY
END FGM
BAR

Electric Pavilion at the corner of Coldharbour Lane and Brixton Road. Now The Ritzy. Circa 1911.

A motorbike with sidecar outside The Ritzy cinema in Brixton Oval. 1978.

View of the Tate Library garden and Lambeth Town Hall.

A snowy evening in the newly redesigned Windrush Square.

◀ End female genital mutilation. Windrush Square.

The true spirit of Brixton. Atlantic Road. 1995.

The corner of Coldharbour Lane and Atlantic Road. ▶

CLOCK
MAKER.
OPTICIAN.
WATCHMAKER
60
SHAVING
HAIR CUTTING
& SHAVING
CIGARETTES
DAVID
58
NESTLE'S
MILK
Brixton

WITH CLARA BOW AND IT PAYS TO ADVERTISE

Brixton Conservative Club member's notice. Effra Social.

Bon Marché shop frontage at the coronation of George VI. 1937.

Officers and committee of Brixton Conservative Club 1978-79. Effra Social.

Metropolitan Police Minstrels at Brixton Theatre. 1921.

◄ The Astoria Cinema Brixton (now Brixton Academy). 1931.

Brixton Synagogue (now Eurolink Business Centre). Opened in 1913 and closed in 1986. Effra Road.

View of St Matthew's Church and Gardens taken from Lambeth Town Hall tower.

'Pure & Juicy' Cooltan Arts party poster. Atlantic Road. 1995.

◀ Ganit - anarchist squatter activist making art installation for metalwork exhibition. Cooltan Arts. 1995.

Lambeth Country Show. 2014.

Music and community in equal shades. We Love Brixton.

Man in the market. He appears to emerge and disappear simultaneously into the environment around him.

Railton Road. 2011.

◂ Flash Pavement Rug. A collaboration between Dolman-Bowles, Eley Kishimoto & 2MZ for We Love Brixton & Transport for London.

Brockwell Hall, Brockwell Park.

The aviary, Brockwell Park.

Lawnmowers in Brockwell Park.

Brockwell Park. 2013.

As the sun rises and sets each day we conquer. Brockwell Park, one of my favourite places in Brixton. ▶

Peace and quiet of a weekday morning at the Lido.

A well dressed stranger at Lambeth Country Show enjoying his morning.

BRIXTON BEACH

In the summer months grass is left to grow, giving a feeling of countryside meadows in the inner city.

These characters where snapped in Brockwell Park at the end of the summer 2010.

The individuals were a representation of that feeling of change and melancholy that the season brings.

Merly rushing through the park on her way to church.

CRAZY

Award-winning Magic Roundabout vegetable sculpture. Lambeth Country Show.

Amy Greenhouse. Lambeth Country Show.

◀ The black knight advances in Lambeth Country Show jousting.

Lunch in Brixton.

The Lambeth Country Show includes a variety of animals, some putting on shows and others being shown.

BCM

◀ Revellers happily undeterred by the rain at the Lambeth Country Show. 2014.

Hootananny ladies' toilet. 2013.

Etchings from the ladies' toilets at Brixton JAMM.

Brixton revellers outside the tube station on their way to Pride. 2015.

The subject is Christina Daniels, who was wrestling with her Brazilian and English identities whilst at The Dogstar on Coldharbour Lane.

One of Brixton's greatest assets is its diversity, where the barriers between age, race and sexuality are blurred. Reclaim Brixton. 2015.

◀ These guys embody a radical form of expression which adds to the rich tapestry of our streets. Reclaim Brixton. 2015.

ISAAC WALTON & Co Ltd
BORWICKS
SALE OF
STOCKLEYS
STOCK

Me and my mate Mike jerkin' a leg to some drum and bass! Street party outside the Effra Hall Tavern. 2012.

Residents of St Agnes Place squat strung a rope across the street to escape from bailiffs' eviction.

Dancing to a Rastafarian drumming group playing at Lambeth Country Show.

An unofficial Golden Jubilee party on Coldharbour Lane. 2002.

◂ Opening of Lambeth Town Hall by the Prince of Wales, the future George V. 1908.

Brixton Splash celebrators at Windrush Square. 2014.

In the early days of Brixton Splash, Wassie One would turn in a fabulous set at the bottom of Atlantic Road.

Early arrival gets Atlantic Road to himself. Splash has become a victim of its own success as numbers increase.

It was a fine, fine moment. As they sometimes say roundabout here: 'Jah Rastafari'.

These musicians can be heard daily on Brixton Road. I love the energy when I walk up the stairs from the station and hear them playing. ▶

Sainsbury's
Local
value
everyday

Dancing outside Judy's Fashions at Brixton Splash. Coldharbour Lane. 2011.

Children compete in a hula-hoop competition. Endymion Road street party. 2010.

◂ Sitting in the street enjoying the last of the evening light. Endymion Road street party. 2010.

Boom Box Fridge. Town Hall Parade.

DMZ parties paved the foundations for a sound which would spread the world over. Dubstep history.

DJ outside United 80. Brixton Village.

It's not a club night, it's cool people, in a cool place, fresh music, but it's not a long ting.

◀ 'No Long Ting', curated by Ty, dubbed South London Party of the year. 2012.

Cyndi and Chris of United 80 DJing during the early days of Snugg in Brixton Village.

Grandmaster Flash on a Dogstar adventure. Coldharbour Lane.

Alabama 3 at their spiritual home of Brixton JAMM.

Basement Jaxx, Brixton Academy. The energy at their home gig was, as always, sensational.

Sold out Kasabian gig at the Academy. Was a great gig in one of London's best venues! 2014.

A physical theatre performance produced by arts organisation The Brick Box in Brixton Village. 2010.

Cubicle cat wants you to be happy. Hootananny ladies toilet. 2013.

The George Canning Pub, later the Hobgoblin, now the Hootananny. ▶

BRIXTON
BRIXTON 3 CAMDEN TOWN
KING
SOAPS
Pears'
SOAP
KINGS
BRIXTON ROAD – KENNINGTON – CHARING + – REGENT STREET – ALBANY STREET
GENERAL
H. Gilbert
The George Canning

Brixton Windmill.

Brixton flour. Windmill Gardens. 2015

The Friends of Windmill Gardens' masterpiece.

BLACK CULTURAL
ARCHIVES MUSEUM
BRIXTON : UK
NORTH KENSINGTON
KENSAL GREEN

Black Cultural Archives first official building on the corner of Atlantic Road and Coldharbour Lane. c2004.

Raleigh Hall building before refurbishment. 2005.

Left to right: Dame Jowell MP, Will Smith, Chukka Umuna MP and Dawn Hill, Chair of BCA Board of Trustees.

The doors open to our new building in Windrush Square on the 24 July 2014.

◄ Black Cultural Archives members marching at Notting Hill Carnival. c1984.

Once a worker for the miners' union, this man still feels comfortable expressing his views on Thatcher.

The models are sisters Indigo and Eliyah Lassen, gorgeous girls who show the beauty you can find in Brixton.

Sam used to be a common face around Brixton but sadly hasn't been seen for a while.

A Present 4 Peace volunteer at the We Love Brixton event.

Block Workout founder Terroll Lewis and crew.

Building the first Block Workout gym.

Block Workout in action.

Block Workout. Somerleyton Road.

Someone finding time to relax in Brixton. ▶

Wearing (we are in) Jamaica.

Brixton street art on a sunny summer's day.

A Brixton local expresses herself in pink. True self-confidence.

Welcome to Brixton – visitors always welcome.

Taken on Elm Park Road. You see the real residents of Brixton in the side streets away from the hustle and bustle.

Our message to a transitional Brixton through the words of our iconic (unimaginatively named) 'man in the hat' mural by local artist Tizer. ▶

SAVE BRIXTON

BRIXTON
iPhone 5c
RELIANCE ARCADE
SHOP
HERE

◀ Long live beautiful Brixton. 2014.

PHOTOGRAPHY CREDITS.

Aliyah Otchere
& Amira Hassan
page: 81.

Amon Brown
page: 39.

Anna Rocchi
pages: 88, 90.

Ayse Hassan
pages: 5, 7, 15, 26, 49, 51, 52, 53, 59, 62, 63, 83, 85, 86, 100, 104, 110, 111, 118, 120, 122, 140, 146, 147, 169, 170.

Bill Linskey
pages: 23, 24, 25, 48, 79, 80, 88, 89, 94, 95, 96, 97, 126, 128, 139, 141, 142, 143, 145, 150, 168, 179, 180.

Billy Macrae
pages: 106, 172, 173.

Black Cultural Archives
pages: 182, 183.

Caitlin Smith
pages: 44, 45, 46, 54, 56, 150.

Chantelle Clarke-Medford
page: 114.

Cristina Dell'Erba
pages: 6, 30, 31.

Dashti Jahfar
pages: 72, 133, 134, 135.

David Bushay
page:192.

David Hoffman
pages: 67, 68, 69.

David McGlashlan
page: 177.

David Sampson
pages: 17, 59, 82, 91, 152, 185.

Elam Forrester
page: 65.

Federico Domenici
pages: 18, 33, 35, 90, 91, 98, 188.

Flo Fairweather
pages: 162, 178.

Georgina Rodgers
page: 169.

Harkaran Gill
pages: 61, 175, 190.

Holly Green
pages: 8, 91, 130.

Janine Weidel
pages: 32, 37, 40, 49, 50, 55, 57, 58, 65, 74, 90, 112, 113, 123, 149, 169.

Jason Alfred-Palmer
pages: 9, 29, 34, 166, 167.

Jerry Tremaine
pages: 80, 102, 159.

Joshua Lindo
page: 151.

Julia Martin
page: 11.

Karin Bultje
pages: 91, 158.

Keanna Williams
& Paula Espeut
page: 27.

Keith Andrews
pages: 19, 47, 49, 70, 85, 86, 87, 123, 124, 129, 137, 189.

Kim Bouwer
pages: 163, 177.

Lambeth Archive
pages: 21, 70, 139, 144.

Laura Ward
pages: 12, 153.

THANKING YOUS.

Jeanine Woollard
David Bushay
Luke Forsythe
Oscar Taylor
Shaan Syed
Miles Byrd
Alex Lewis
Ted & Ted
Paul Scott
Lizzy King
Tom Doyle
Chris Hughes
Keith Andrews
Gavin Bambrick
Monique Brown
Mr & Mrs Woollard
Pins
Bill Linskey
Mike Urban
John Curran
Chris Ellesse
Brian Leonard
Claire Atherton
The Taylor Family

NEW ENTRIES.

We have started the Great Brixton story, it's for all of us to continue. Have you, friends or family got any images you'd like to submit for future volumes? Send your entries to **photos@greatbrixton.com** - alternatively we'll happily scan them. Please email us first to arrange an appointment.

All images featured in the publication will be fully credited and remain the property of the owner. Your images will be treated with the utmost care and will not be used for commercial gain.

f TheGreatBrixtonProject

@TheGreatBrixton

GREAT BRIXTON CREDITS.

Publisher	The Champion Agency
Creative Director	Scott Leonard
Co-curators	Miranda Hutton
	David Bushay
	Scott Leonard
Art Director	David Bushay
Designer	Flo Fairweather
Junior Designer	Felix Belger
Project Manager	Oscar Taylor
Producer	Conor Jones
Editor	Richard Nield